For Doris and George
– A.H.B.

For Matthew and Sally
– J.C.

Published in 1996 by Magi Publications
22 Manchester Street, London W1M 5PG

Text © 1996 A.H.Benjamin
Illustrations © 1996 Jane Chapman

A.H.Benjamin and Jane Chapman have asserted their rights
to be identified as the author and illustrator of this work under the
Copyright, Designs and Patents Act, 1988.

Printed and bound in Belgium by Proost N.V. Turnhout

ISBN 1 85430 402 X

What if?

by A.H.Benjamin

illustrated by Jane Chapman

Something special was happening on Buttercup Farm.
The farmer had brought a kangaroo back with him
from Australia.
It was arriving that very day!
All the animals gathered in the farmyard to talk
about it. They had never seen a kangaroo before.

"What can a kangaroo do,
anyway?" they asked.
But nobody knew.

"What if she can crow?" asked Rooster. "What if she gets up very early and crows so loudly that she wakes the whole farm? Perhaps she will even count the hens and chicks to see if any are missing. The farmer won't need me any more then, and I will have to look for another job. *Cock-a-doodle-doo!* Perhaps I won't even find one!"

"What if she can herd sheep?" said Dog. "What if she rounds them all up, and takes them to graze on the highest and greenest hills? She might even chase a fox or two. The farmer will be so pleased with her that he will send me off to live in the kennels. *Bow-wow!* I would hate that!"

"How horrible!"

said everyone.

"What if she can catch mice?" said Cat.
"What if she catches all the mice in the barn
and a few rats, too? Maybe even the spiders
would be scared to live there. Then the
farmer would get rid of me,
and I would become a stray,
foraging for food in dustbins.
Miaow! I'd miss my milk
and sardines!"

"How awful!"

said everyone.

"What if she can give milk?" said Cow. "What if she fills up all the churns in the farm with such rich, creamy milk that people will rush to buy it? Then nobody would want mine, and the farmer would make me pull the heavy plough instead. *Moo!* I couldn't stand that!"

"How shocking!"

said everyone.

"What if she can grow wool?" said Sheep.
"What if she has a thick, woolly fleece,
whiter than snow and softer than silk?
And maybe her coat will grow twice
as fast as mine. The farmer would be so
delighted, that *my* wool would only be
used to stuff old pillows and cushions.
Baa! I wouldn't let them come near me
with their shears!"

"How terrible!"
said everyone.

"What if she can pull a cart?" said Horse.
"What if she takes a cartful of fruit and
vegetables to the market and gets there
a lot quicker than I could? She might
even give rides to the farmer's children.
There would be no place for me here then,
and I would end up in an old horses' home.
Neigh! I'm too young for that!"

"How frightful!"

said everyone.

The animals were very, very worried.
They were so busy worrying they did not notice
that some of the young ones had strayed away.
"Where are my puppies?" asked Dog,
looking around.

"And my kittens?" asked Cat.
Sheep could not find her tiny lamb, either.

All the animals searched and
searched, but not a kitten, nor
a puppy, nor a tiny lamb could
they find anywhere.
They looked from the barn . . .

. . . to the pigsty, with no luck.
"This is dreadful!" crowed Rooster.
"Horrible!" woofed Dog.
"Awful!" miaowed Cat.

"Shocking!" mooed Cow.
"Terrible!" baaed Sheep.
"Frightful!" neighed Horse.
Suddenly, across the field they saw . . .

. . . a very strange animal indeed, leaping and bounding towards them.

"Hello," it said. "I'm Kangaroo!"

The animals stopped searching
for their babies.
They stared and stared.
For the funny-looking animal
had a big pouch in her tummy,
and in the pouch . . .

. . . were
three kittens,
two puppies
and
one tiny lamb!

"I've found your babies," said Kangaroo.
"I'm a baby minder. I look after the young,
and carry them when their little feet get tired.
They love it!"
"*What a good idea!*" the animals cried.
And crowing and barking and miaowing and
mooing and baaing and neighing, they all
welcomed Kangaroo to her new home.